D1218962

Bigger Than a Baby

By Harriet Ziefert   Pictures by Laura Rader

HarperCollins*Publishers*

For Emma

For Sam

For Anna

Bigger Than a Baby
Text copyright © 1991 by Harriet Ziefert
Illustrations copyright © 1991 by Laura Rader
Printed in Singapore for Harriet Ziefert, Inc.
1 2 3 4 5 6 7 8 9 10
First Edition

Library of Congress Cataloging-in-Publication Data
Ziefert, Harriet.
  Bigger than a baby / by Harriet Ziefert ; pictures by
Laura Rader.
     p.   cm.
  Summary: Simple text and illustrations explain how
children grow physically and emotionally.
  ISBN 0-06-026902-2.—ISBN 0-06-026903-0 (lib. bdg.)
  1. Child development—Juvenile literature. [1. Babies.
2. Growth. 3. Child development.] I. Rader, Laura, ill.
II. Title.
HQ767.9.Z53   1991   90-20287
305.23′1—dc20   CIP
                                           AC

CONTENTS

Growing
All living things grow. Animals grow.

A kitten grows—
and becomes a cat.

A chick grows—
and becomes a hen.

A lamb grows—
and becomes a sheep.

A calf grows—
and becomes a cow.

People grow, too.

A girl baby grows up and becomes a woman.

A boy baby grows up and becomes a man.

How Babies Begin

A baby begins when a sperm from a father joins with an egg from a mother. The baby grows inside the mother's womb for nine months. Then it's time for it to be born.

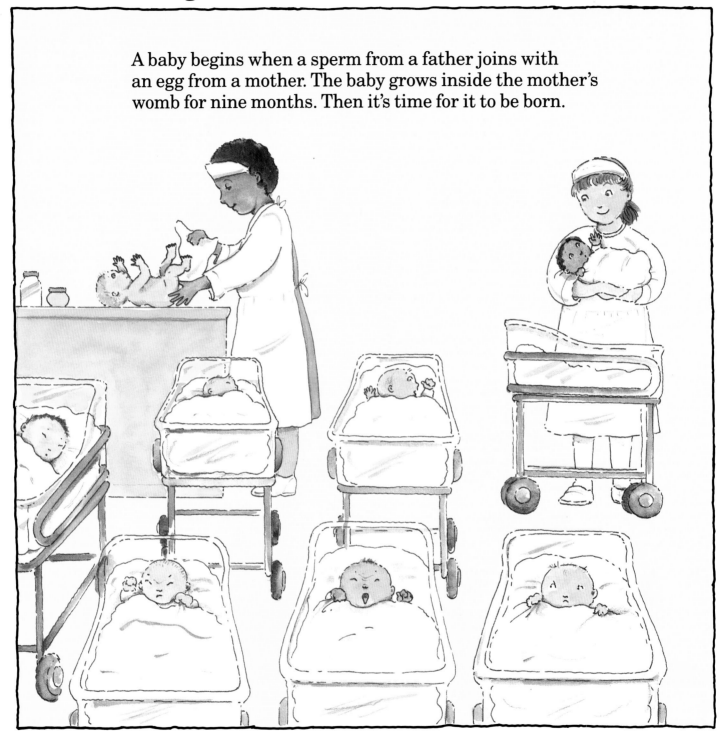

Newborn babies are very little.

They sleep.

They cry.

They suck.

They burp.

A Baby Learns

In the first months of life, a newborn baby learns:

To turn and look.

To gaze at faces.

To babble and coo.

To smile.

The baby also learns:

When you move your hand toward your mouth, you can suck your thumb.

When you put your feet in the air, you can play with your toes.

When you twist your body, you can roll over.

When you shut your eyes, it gets dark.

Look at a Baby

3 months

6 months

9 months

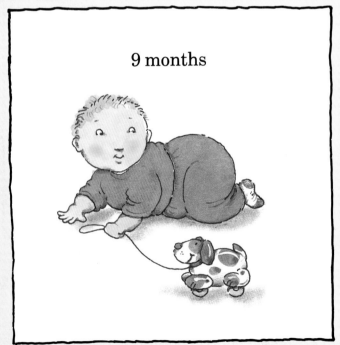

12 months

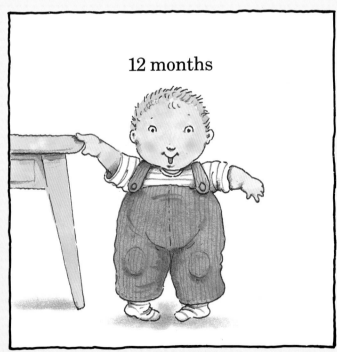

In just one year, a baby can grow three times the size he was when he was born.

Sometimes it's hard to tell which baby is a boy and which baby is a girl. But if you look at their bodies, you can see the difference.

All babies pee and poop in their diapers.

Lots of growing has to happen before a baby is ready to use a potty.

This baby is trying to tell its mother something—but lots of growing has to happen before the baby can tell her in words.

You're Different from a Baby

A baby doesn't understand that a mommy who goes out will come back.

But you know your mommy will come back. So you can have a good time with the babysitter.

A baby who's hungry wants to eat right away.

But you can wait for your dinner.

You might not like to wait for a drink, but you can do it.

You can wait your turn.

But a baby can't.

You can wait for the future.

You can wait for a visit to Grandma's.

You can wait for your birthday.

And you can wait for Christmas.

You can plan for the future, too.

You can save pennies so you can buy a new ball.

You can practice soccer so you can make the team.

You can pack a backpack, so you'll have toys to play with when you get to Grandma's house.

A Body Grows   Your body has grown a lot since you were a baby.

A baby doctor can tell a mommy how much
her baby has grown since birth.

You are getting taller, but unless someone weighs and measures
you, you probably don't notice how much you are growing.

When Aunt Tillie comes to visit and says,

"My, how you've grown!
I remember you when…"

that's when you know it!

Ways you can tell your body is growing and changing:

Your jeans won't button.

Your party shoes pinch your toes.

Your sleeves are too short.

Your bike's too small.

Your hair, nails, bones, muscles, teeth—everything is growing all the time.

Your hair grows about an inch every month. When it gets too long, you can get a haircut.

Your fingernails and toenails grow, too. When they get too long, someone has to clip them.

Big teeth grow under your baby teeth until they push them out. First you have a loose tooth, then a big space, then a new tooth!

Your Mind Grows   Your mind has grown a lot since you were a baby.

A baby likes books—
to tear and to chew!

But you can read the pictures.
And some words, too.

A baby likes crayons—
to touch and to taste!

But you can use them
to write and to draw.

You know that five apples are five apples if you…

line them up…

pile them up…

or put them in a bag.

Everyone's mind is growing. And everyone is always learning.

Feelings As you get older, you can put your feelings into words.

"You make me so mad."

"I miss you."

"I'm happy."

"I'm embarrassed."

"I love you."

"I hate you."

"I'm excited."

"I'm scared."

You learn to understand your feelings and other people's feelings.

You can have an argument.

You can be friends again.

You can decide to be alone.

You can decide to be with a friend.

27

You may not remember what you were like when you were a baby.

You looked at books upside down.

Your favorite game was peek-a-boo.

You ate with your fingers.

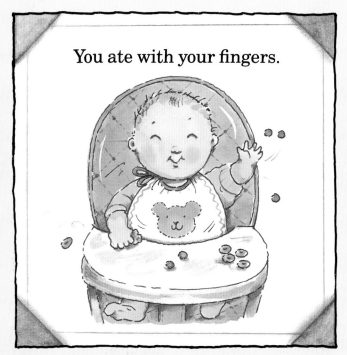

You weren't embarrassed to be naked.

Now you can look at old photos to see what you were like.

Your five senses helped you learn about the world.

You tasted it. You smelled it. You touched it. You looked at it. You listened to it.

Bigger Than a Baby

You've learned a lot about the world.

You can understand what you were like when you were little.

You can imagine what it may be like when you get bigger.

All living things grow, but only people can
remember the past and plan for the future.